"To my amazing parents,
who gave me the courage to try new things and
always encouraged me to chase my dreams.
I love you both to the moon and back!"

– Cheryl Johnson

This book is given with love

To:

_____

From:

_____

Gaya & Papa

Summer 2022

We ♡ Birds and We ♡ U!

Words + Facts To Know

Habitats

| Grasslands | Beaches & Coastlines | Ponds & Lakes | Marshes | Trees & Forests | Bushes & Shrubs |

A "habitat" is the physical surroundings where the bird lives. A habitat is made up of several physical factors such as the type of plants that are around or if there's water in the area. Habitats are often identified by the most common plant in the area or a physical feature such as grass or lakes.

Migration

"Migration" refers to the regular movement of birds from one location to another. Migration often happens during different seasons and is marked in this book using diagrams like the one to the left.

Where birds can be found

Where birds can *not* be found

Are You Ready For An AMAZING Birding Adventure?

You'll discover most things in nature have a pretty interesting tale to tell once you start looking, and birds are certainly no exception.

There are over 9,500 different species of birds in the world. In the United States, there are over 800 different birds that either pass through on the way to their winter or summer homes or decide to hang out and stay a while.

With so many species to choose from, it was hard to narrow it down, but these are some of the "amazing stars" of the United States birding world.

So, let's go meet a few of these feathery creatures, learn a little more about them, and see what makes them so incredibly amazing!

Want to Learn More About Birds?

Merlin Phone App:

Identify a bird with a photo, or if you don't have a photo, it will ask you 5 simple questions to help you figure out what the bird is.

Websites:

www.AllAboutBirds.org

www.ebird.org

www.FeederWatch.org

Atlantic Puffin

An Atlantic Puffin's favorite food is fish and their bodies are perfectly made to catch them! Puffins can fly, but they are better swimmers than flyers. When they dive underwater, they use their wings like flippers and their webbed feet to steer in the direction of the fish. Puffins can stay underwater for up to 60 seconds and can dive up to 200 feet deep looking for fish. 200 feet is almost as tall as a 10-story building!

Amazing Swimmers!

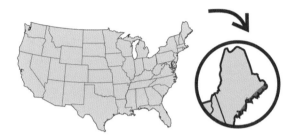

Spring & Summer

Atlantic Puffins spend almost all of their lives floating around the Atlantic Ocean. In fact, the only time they come on land is in the spring and summer when they start their family. They make their nests on the rocky ledges of cliffs in Maine and Canada. Baby Puffins are called "Pufflings."

Atlantic Puffins are small, stocky birds that spend most of their lives at sea. They look a lot like penguins with their black and white bodies and bright orange and black bills, but Puffins and Penguins aren't related at all. Male and female Puffins have the same coloring, but the males are usually a little larger than the females. Some people call them the "Clowns of the Sea."

Height
10 Inches = Vase

Weight
14 ounces = Soccer Ball

Habitat
Beaches & Coastlines

Black Skimmer

Black Skimmers are the only bird in the United States whose bill has an upper mandible is shorter than its lower mandible. They feed by "skimming" along the water, dipping their lower mandible into the water, and snapping it shut when they feel they've caught a fish. When Black Skimmers are born, the lower and upper parts of their bill are the same size, but as they grow, the lower bill grows faster and longer.

Amazing Bills!

Spring & Summer

Black Skimmers love living at the beach. They like to hang out with other Black Skimmers in a group called a colony, so if you see one, there are probably others close by. Unlike many birds who are active only during the day, Black Skimmers will often look for food both in the day and in the night but are most active in the early morning and late evening.

Black Skimmers are coastal birds that eat small fish, shrimp, and other creatures that live in water. When they are looking for food, they will fly very close to the water but just high enough so their wings don't get wet. When they are tired, they will sometimes lie down on the ground. If you see them like this, you might think that they are hurt, but don't worry, they're just resting and enjoying a nap.

Height
17 Inches = Blender

Weight
12 Ounces = Soup Can

Habitat
Beaches & Coastlines

Common Nighthawk

Common Nighthawks are great flyers and can eat up to 500 mosquitoes a day. If you see one flying about looking for mosquitoes, you might think it's a bat because it doesn't fly smoothly. They will suddenly change direction, zig-zagging across the sky as they chase bugs around. Because of this nighttime, zig-zagging flying motion, some people refer to them as "bull bats."

Amazing Mosquito Catchers!

Spring & Summer

In the early morning and evening, you can see Common Nighthawks zipping around the sky chasing mosquitoes. At night, you might even find them weaving under light posts searching for bugs. Listen for them making their distinctive "meeep meeep" sound as they fly.

During the day, they will nap in trees and sometimes nap out in the open on posts, roads, and fields that are in quiet areas. Common Nighthawks are cute birds with huge eyes and little beaks that open up into a huge mouth, both of which help them to find and catch their prey. When they sit in a tree (perching), they are one of the few birds that perch in the same direction as what they are sitting on.

Height
8 Inches = Banana

Weight
2 Ounces = Tennis Ball

Habitat
Trees & Forests

European Starling

Birds that have not always lived in an area but have been brought in from another location are called "introduced species." European Starlings are birds that you can see all over the United States, but they've only lived here for about 130 years. There are millions of European Starlings in the United States, and all of them are descended from the 100+ birds that were released in New York City in the 1890s.

Amazing History!

Year Round

European Starlings are very common birds and can be found almost anywhere, even in neighborhoods and parks. They eat seeds and small insects so they will often hop around the grass in fields and lawns looking for food. They often travel in groups with other types of black birds such as Grackles and Cowbirds.

If you put out suet (a mixture of solid fat or lard, seeds, and even peanut butter), you might have them visit your backyard. European Starlings get their name because in the Fall and Winter, the tips of their purple, blue, and green feathers turn white making it look like their bodies are covered in stars. In the spring and summer, the white and gold tips of their feathers fade so they look solid black, but in the sun, their feathers still shimmer with green and purple.

Height
8 Inches = Banana

Weight
3.5 Ounces = Deck of Cards

Habitat
Grasslands

Greater Prairie-Chicken

When a male Greater Prairie-Chicken is trying to find a girlfriend, he will lean forward, pop up his head feathers, fill up the bright yellow sacks on the side of his head with air, stomp his feet around like he's dancing, and call for the females to notice him. This is called "booming." Each year, for hundreds of years, these birds return to the same place, called a "lek," to do their dance.

Amazing Dancers!

Year Round

Greater Prairie-Chickens eat seeds and both live and raise their babies on the ground, so they like large, open fields with tall grass. In Texas, near Houston, there is the Attwater Prairie Chicken National Wildlife Refuge, a place designed especially for these amazing birds.

Back in the 1800s, there were millions of Greater Prairie-Chickens that lived on the plains in the central United States from North Dakota all the way into Texas. Now there are almost none left because people have turned the birds' habitat into towns and fields for crops. Luckily, lots of people have been working to create new places for these birds to live so that, hopefully, their numbers will increase and we will be able to enjoy them for years to come.

Height

17 Inches = Blender

Weight

2 Pounds = 2 Footballs

Habitat

Grasslands

Killdeer

Killdeers, unlike other birds, don't build nests. Instead, they lay their eggs in an open area, usually in a space with lots of rocks so that the eggs blend in, but sometimes they will even lay their eggs on a street or in a driveway. If a predator such as other birds, animals, and even people get too close to the eggs, the parents will pretend to have a broken wing to try to draw the predator away from the eggs.

Amazing Parents!

Year Round

Killdeers eat snails, beetles, grasshoppers, and other bugs, so you can often see them looking for food in parking lots, on lawns, in parks, and in open fields. They are very comfortable living around people, so don't be surprised if you see one looking for food in your yard or local park.

Killdeers are considered "shore birds" (birds that live around water) even though they don't live or nest near water. The males and females look alike. Unlike many baby birds, baby Killdeers look a lot like their parents from the moment they are born and they can walk out of the nest as soon as their feathers are dry. If the babies get scared, they will crawl under their parents' body to snuggle and hide in their mother's or father's chest feathers.

Height
10 Inches = iPad

Weight
3.5 Ounces = Deck of Cards

Habitat
Grasslands

Loggerhead Shrike

Have you ever noticed a grasshopper, dragonfly, or lizard stabbed onto a barbed wire or chain link fence? Chances are that you're seeing a Loggerhead Shrike at work. These amazing birds will catch a meal and stab it onto a piece of wire to not only hold the prey still while the bird eats, but to save any leftovers for later. If an insect is poisonous, the bird will leave it for a few days until the poison goes away and it's safe to eat.

Amazing Eaters!

Spring & Summer

Fall & Winter

Loggerhead Shrikes feed on small bugs, reptiles, rodents, and birds. You can often find them sitting on fences, tree branches, and power lines as they look for something they can swoop down and grab for a meal. You might see them in your neighborhood, but they are more common near fields and parks.

Loggerhead Shrikes are songbirds that act like birds of prey. They have a sharp, curved tip on their bill, like hawks, that helps them to tear their food apart and eat it. They are very strong birds and can carry things, such as other birds, that weigh as much as they do. Because of the way they catch and stab their food, some people call Loggerhead Shrikes "butcher birds."

Height
8 Inches = Banana

Weight
1.5 Ounces = 100 Paperclips

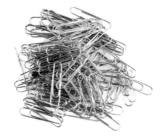

Habitat
Grasslands

Northern Mockingbird

They are referred to as "mimics." This means they copy and sing the songs and calls of other birds. A male Northern Mockingbird can learn over 200 different songs during his lifetime. Males will sing all day long and sometimes even during the night, but they sing more often on nights when there's a full moon. Mockingbirds know so many songs that they can sing for hours without repeating themselves.

Amazing Singers!

Year Round

Northern Mockingbirds are common residents in trees and bushes in neighborhoods and parks all over the United States. You can find them bouncing around tree branches or lawns looking for bugs or sitting on top of a tree singing one of their many different songs.

Northern Mockingbirds aren't afraid of much! It's not uncommon for them to even attack a cat if they feel threatened. If a cat gets too close, the bird will quickly swoop down, peck at it, and swoop away until the cat moves on. Northern Mockingbirds eat a little bit of everything, including insects and fruit, but they are not a bird that will come to a backyard feeder.

Height
9 Inches = Vase

Weight
2 Ounces = Tennis Ball

Habitat
Trees & Forests

Pileated Woodpecker

Because they look for food and make nests by "drilling" into trees with their bill, their heads are specially made so they don't get headaches from all that tapping. Also, their tongues are twice as long as their bills so they can reach deep into nooks and crannies to get at bugs that might be hiding deep in the tree bark. And because its tongue is sticky, it can pull those insects right out of their hiding places.

Amazing Heads!

Year Round

Pileated Woodpeckers eat ants and other insects that live in bark, so you can find them in forests, parks, or neighborhoods with lots of tall trees. If you put out some suet, they might visit your backyard feeders. These woodpeckers are very shy, so you might hear them first before you see them. Listen for a loud tapping sound and their "wuk wuk wuk" call.

Pileated Woodpeckers are the largest woodpecker in the United States. The male and the female look very similar, except the male has a red stripe that runs along his chin and the red feathers on the top of his head extend all the way to his bill, like the bird in the photo. They will make a nest by using their bill to "drill a hole" in the side of a tree. Pileated Woodpeckers use their nests for only one season, so other birds will move into the empty nest the next year.

Height
17 Inches = Blender

Weight
12 Ounces = Soup Can

Habitat
Trees & Forests

Reddish Egret

These birds are probably the most entertaining and dramatic species to watch when they are looking for food. They will zip back and forth around a shallow shoreline or pond, whipping their head around and flapping their wings. When they see a fish, they will raise up their wings and plunge their head into the water to grab their lunch. Scientists believe they do this to confuse the fish, making them easier to catch.

Amazing Hunters!

Year Round

Since Reddish Egrets eat small fish, frogs, and shrimp; you can find them feeding or just relaxing along the shore of a beach or in small ponds and marshes. Reddish Egrets are large shorebirds that live, eat, and nest near water. The males and females look similar, so it's hard to tell them apart.

This species has two very different color patterns. One is called a "dark morph" and its body is a light grey while its head and neck are a rusty red. The other is called a "white morph" and is entirely white. Both the dark and white morph have brownish bills with black tips. In the spring, when they are looking for a mate, their bills will turn a bright pink color.

Height
30 Inches = Table

Weight
14 Ounces = Football

Habitat
Ponds & Lakes

Rock Wren

Not many creatures can survive without water, but Rock Wrens can! These amazing little birds live in very dry areas, like deserts, where there's not much rainfall so there often isn't a lot of water around. Rock Wrens, like many creatures, have adapted to their environment. Their favorite food is made up of insects and spiders and their bodies are able to get all the water they need from these bugs.

Amazing Survivalists!

Year Round

Can you guess where Rock Wrens live based on their name? If you guessed in rocky areas, you'd be right! These cute little birds live and build their nests in rock crevices, hidden from predators. If you want to try and spot one, sometimes they will make little trails of rocks leading up to their nest.

They like to sing and can know up to a hundred different songs, so you will probably hear them before you see them. If you live in or visit a dry, desert area, there's a good chance that you might see a Rock Wren, though it will be hard to tell the males and females apart since they look so similar. Some of these birds live all year in the same location while others will fly north in the spring to start and raise a family.

Height
5 Inches = iPhone

Weight
0.6 Ounces = AAA Battery

Habitat
Bushes & Shrubs

Scissor-Tailed Flycatcher

Scissor-Tailed Flycatchers eat small bugs and insects. They will fly around and catch their food or pounce on insects on the ground. They use their long tails to help them change direction quickly while flying, so those poor little bugs don't stand a chance of escaping. A male's tail feathers can be up to 9" long and a female's tail feathers can be up to 6" long.

Amazing Acrobats!

Spring & Summer

Scissor-Tailed Flycatchers like to wander and have been seen all throughout the United States. They are commonly found in the spring and summer in the central part of the United States and spend their winters in South America. When they are getting ready to migrate, they will gather in large flocks before they leave.

You can find them in open areas, sitting up high in trees, or along fences looking for bugs that they can swoop down and grab. Scissor-Tailed Flycatchers might be one of the most amazing-looking birds you'll ever see. When they are young, they look like most other birds with normal-length tails, but as they grow, their tail feathers lengthen into a long, forked tail. Both the male and female look alike, and both have the long tails that make them so interesting.

Height
14 Inches = Shoebox

Weight
1.5 Ounces = 100 Paperclips

Habitat
Grasslands

Turkey Vulture

If you or I tried to eat something that died and was stinky and smelly, we'd get very sick, but a Turkey Vulture's body is made to protect them from getting sick from any germs that might be living in what they eat. It's their strong stomaches and immune system that are to thank, keeping them safe from the germs and bacteria that live in decaying animals.

Amazing Bodies!

Spring & Summer

Fall & Winter

Because of what they eat, Turkey Vultures live just about everywhere, including the city and the country. If you look up in the sky, you can often see Turkey and Black Vultures soaring and circling around looking for food or just enjoying a nice sunny day together.

Turkey Vultures are large birds that are part of nature's clean up crew! If an animal dies, they literally fly in and clean up the mess. They have an amazing sense of smell that helps them find dead animals. This might sound gross, but Turkey Vultures help keep things clean. Think of them as nature's garbage collectors.

Height
30 Inches = Table

Weight
3 Pounds = 3 Soccer Balls

Habitat
Trees & Forests

Verdin

Most birds live in a nest only when they are raising a family, but Verdins live in a nest all year long and have different nests depending on the time of the year. In winter, their nests are thicker and built with thousands of twigs that help them stay warm when it gets cold. In summer, the nests are thinner and face the direction that the wind blows to help the nest stay cool.

Amazing Nest Builders!

Year Round

Verdins like hot, dry areas with lots of little, scrubby bushes. They move very fast around trees and bushes as they look for food. Sometimes you can see them sitting on the top of a tree or bush singing their beautiful song. They are one of the smallest birds that live in the United States.

Verdins have a yellow face and a black stripe that makes them look like they are wearing a mask. The males and the females look alike with light grey bodies, darker grey backs, and a little red patch on their wings. Their favorite meal is small bugs, spiders, and berries. Sometimes they will hang upside down from the branches of trees and bushes trying to catch a bug to eat.

Height
4 Inches = Mug

Weight
0.2 Ounces = Quarter

Habitat
Bushes & Shrubs

White Pelican

White Pelicans love a good meal of fresh fish! A White Pelican's lower bill is loose and stretchy and can hold up to three gallons of water, that's the same size as three, big containers of milk! They will use their bill like a bucket to scoop up water and fish then close their bill, dip their head down to let the water drain out, and swallow the fish.

Amazing Fishermen!

Spring & Summer

Fall & Winter

In the winter, White Pelicans can be found in the Southern United States floating around in the ocean near the shore and in small lakes. During the summer, they fly north to the Northern United States and Canada to raise their family. In spring and fall, you might see a group of White Pelicans flying above you. Look for their white bodies with black wings.

White Pelicans are one of the largest birds that you'll see in the United States. They can weigh as much as a bowling ball and when they fly, their wings can be up to nine feet across! White pelicans always enjoy a tasty meal of fresh fish and will float around the water waiting for their dinner to swim by so they can snatch it up.

Height
50 Inches = Flat-screen TV

Weight
15 Pounds = Bowling Ball

Habitat
Beaches & Coastlines

Wood Duck

In the winter and spring, the feathers of the male Wood Duck look like a rainbow, with all sorts of beautiful colors. If you see them in the sunshine, they almost seem to sparkle. From late summer to early fall, the males lose all of their bright and pretty feathers in a process called "molting." Their new feathers make them look just like a female Wood Duck. The change of feather colors is called "Eclipse Plumage."

Amazing Color Changes!

Year Round

Like other ducks, Wood Ducks can be found near and in water, eating the plants and bugs. Their favorite places to be are ponds, slow moving streams, or marshy areas with lots of cattails that they can hide in if they feel scared or threatened.

Wood Ducks might be the prettiest ducks we have in the United States. They were given their name because of where they like to make their nests...in trees! Plus, they are one of the few ducks that have webbed feet with strong claws so they can perch on tree branches without falling off. If you ever visit a pond or lake and see what looks like big bird houses attached to the tree trunks, there's a good chance that they are duck boxes for Wood Ducks to nest in.

Height
20 Inches = Mirror

Weight
22 Ounces = Basketball

Habitat
Ponds & Lakes

Yellow Warbler

Like most warblers, Yellow Warblers spend the winters in South America and fly north for the spring and summer. This is called "migration," and when they migrate, they will leave South America and fly all night over the Gulf of Mexico on their way to the United States. That's hundreds of miles over water all in one night! Can you imagine flapping your arms all night? Phew, that would be exhausting!

Amazing Flyers!

Spring & Summer

Yellow Warblers are one of the most common warblers that live in the United States. They like areas where they can find their favorite foods, small insects and spiders, so look for them in bushes and areas near streams and marshes. During migration in April and May, you can see them throughout the United States.

Yellow Warblers are small birds with bright yellow bodies. The males and females look similar, but the male is a brighter yellow and has darker brown streaks on his chest. They are active little birds that like to jump around branches in bushes and shrubs looking for snacks. If you want to go out looking for warblers and other birds, remember that they are more active and easier to spot in the mornings and evenings.

Height
5 Inches = iPhone

Weight
0.2 Ounces = Quarter

Habitat
Bushes & Shrubs

About the Author

Cheryl Johnson started on her "birding" journey in 2016. She has had a wonderful time learning about nature, discovering the incredible beauty that surrounds us, meeting lots of other fellow enthusiasts, and developing her skills and knowledge as a photographer and naturalist.

She stumbled upon wildlife photography by chance when she joined a bird walk through a local park as part of a magazine story she was writing and instantly fell in love with it! So, she grabbed her camera and prepared to take some "award-winning" photos of our fine, feathered friends because, really, how difficult could photographing birds really be? She soon discovered the answer: incredibly difficult! Not to be bested by the tiny, feathered creatures, she decided to figure out how it was done, and an obsession was born!

Cheryl started by purchasing feeders and photographing the birds visiting her backyard and soon found herself wandering all over town, up and down beaches, through forests, and all over the state snapping pictures of everything that flew past her lens.

Cheryl's award-winning photography has been featured in several publications, marketing campaigns, and websites. Her art has been displayed in several businesses: The Five Points Museum of Contemporary Art and the Victoria Art League in Victoria, Texas. She's also been a guest speaker sharing her passion with many groups and organizations. When not traveling all over the state, country, and world photographing birds and other wildlife, she lives in Victoria, Texas, with her husband, two daughters, and her dog.

See Cheryl's Other Books:

"My Backyard Bird Book"
"My Book of Plumology"
"My Bird Scavenger Hunt"

Visit Cheryl's Website:

www.CherylJohnsonAuthor.com
for more information
and photography

Amazing Junior Ornithologist

Having completed the necessary course study, this is to certify that

 X

_____

is an official Junior Ornithologist.

"May birds of a feather stick together!"

 **Claim Your FREE Gift!**

Visit ➡ <u>PDICBooks.com/Gift</u>

Thank you for purchasing My Amazing Bird Book, and welcome to the Puppy Dogs & Ice Cream family.

We're certain you're going to love the little gift we've prepared for you at the website above.